The Alchemy of Love

Turning the Ordinary into the Extraordinary

by

Ujunwa Miriam Ekeh

Oko Obasi

Obasi Reloaded Publishing Inc.
ISBN: 9798862576030
Imprint: Independently published
First edition: 2023
Printed in the United States of America.
Cover design by Oko Obasi

Dedication

To My Parents, Mr. and Mrs. Titus Ekeh,

You have been the unwavering pillars of love in my life, the steadfast beacons of affection that have illuminated my path from the very beginning. Your love has been a guiding force, an unbreakable bond that has nurtured and sustained me through every twist and turn of my journey.

In you both, I have witnessed the epitome of love—selfless, enduring, and boundless. Your love has taught me the value of compassion, the strength of unity, and the beauty of unwavering support. It has been the foundation upon which I have built my life, a source of inspiration that continues to shape my character and values.

Through the highs and lows, you have shown me the transformative power of love. In your embrace, I have found solace and encouragement, and in your wisdom, I have discovered the profound lessons of empathy and understanding. Your love has been a gift beyond measure, and I dedicate the exploration of love to you, the two people who have exemplified its extraordinary nature.

With boundless gratitude and love,

Ujunwa Miriam Ekeh
Umuahia, Nigeria
September, 2023

Acknowledgments

I would like to express my heartfelt gratitude to the individuals who played instrumental roles in the creation of this book. Without their support, wisdom, and unwavering encouragement, this journey into the exploration of love would not have been possible.

To my beloved husband, Mr. Chinomso Kingsley Emeize: Your love has been both my inspiration and my sanctuary throughout this writing process. Your patience, understanding, and unwavering belief in me have been the driving force behind this endeavor. You are not just my life partner but also my biggest supporter, and I am eternally grateful for your presence in my life.

To my esteemed co-author, Dr. Oko Obasi: Collaborating with you has been an enriching and enlightening experience. Your insights, expertise, and dedication to this project have elevated it to new heights. Your willingness to embark on this literary journey with me has made the exploration of love a truly collaborative and fulfilling endeavor.

Your contributions have left an indelible mark on this work, and I am honored to have shared this creative process with you.

I would also like to extend my gratitude to my friends, family, and colleagues, whose encouragement and support have provided me with the inspiration and motivation to pursue this project.

To everyone who has played a part, no matter how small, in the creation of this book, I offer my sincere thanks. Your belief in the power of love and in the importance of its exploration has enriched this work beyond measure.

With heartfelt appreciation,

Ujunwa Miriam Ekeh
Umuahia, Nigeria
September, 2023

Table of Contents

- How love redefines our sense of self and identity.
- Discovering hidden talents and passions through love.
- Overcoming fears and limitations with the power of love.

Chapter 5: Love in Relationships
- The influence of love on our interactions with others.
- Love as a means of resolving conflicts and forging bonds.
- How love transcends the ordinary and touches the sublime.

Chapter 6: Love in Everyday Life
- Examples of love's manifestation in art, music, literature, and nature.
- How love enriches our lives with beauty, joy, and wonder.
- Recognizing the extraordinary within the ordinary.

Chapter 7: Love's Challenges and Triumphs
- The obstacles love often encounters and its capacity to triumph over adversity.
- Lessons learned from love's challenges and growth opportunities.
- The enduring resilience of love.

Chapter 8: The Alchemy of Long-lasting Love
- The qualities and foundations of love that withstand the test of time.
- Navigating life's seasons and maintaining passion in long-lasting relationships.
- Creating milestones and traditions to strengthen love's bond.

Chapter 9: Love's Legacy
- The ripple effect of love and its impact on individuals and communities.
- Love's role in nurturing future generations and inspiring societal change.
- The enduring legacy of love in shaping the world.

Conclusion
- Reflecting on the profound and lasting impact of love.
- Embracing the transformative power of love in all its forms.

About the Author
- Brief introduction to the author, Ujunwa Miriam Ekeh, and her background and passions.

References
- Citations and sources for the content presented in the book.

Preface

Love, in all its forms and manifestations, is a subject that has fascinated and perplexed humanity for as long as we have existed. It is both our most intimate and our most universal experience, an emotion that transcends time, culture, and circumstance. It is at once our greatest source of joy and our deepest well of vulnerability. Love is a force that shapes our individual journeys, molds our relationships, and has the power to transform the world.

In the following pages, we embark on a journey into the extraordinary nature of love. This exploration is not an attempt to define love definitively, for it eludes rigid definitions. Instead, it is an invitation to delve into the depths of this profound human experience, to understand its myriad forms, and to appreciate the beauty and complexity it brings to our lives.

Our journey begins by unraveling the mysteries of love—its hidden magic, the alchemical elements that compose it, and its ability to heal both our emotional and physical wounds. We will witness how love has the power to transform individuals and relationships, fostering personal growth and inspiring compassion.

As we delve deeper, we will explore the diverse forms of love, from the passionate intensity of romantic love to the steadfast bonds of familial and platonic love, and the foundational importance of self-love. Love is not a one-dimensional emotion; it is a multifaceted gem, each facet reflecting a unique facet of affection and connection.

Yet, love is not without its challenges. We will confront the obstacles that love often encounters, from communication breakdowns to external pressures, and learn how enduring love can triumph over adversity. Love's capacity to endure and thrive in the face of challenges is a testament to its resilience.

Our journey culminates with a reflection on love's legacy—a legacy that extends far beyond our individual lives. Love leaves an indelible mark on our relationships, communities, and society, shaping the world and inspiring future generations.

Throughout this exploration, we will draw upon stories, insights, and the collective wisdom of humanity. We will hear from those who have experienced the transformative power of love firsthand and have left a lasting legacy of kindness and compassion in their wake.

As we navigate the pages that follow, let us do so with open hearts and minds, for love is a subject that defies easy categorization or explanation. It is an experience that each of us encounters in our own unique way, and it continues to evolve and shape our lives.

May this journey into the extraordinary nature of love inspire you to cherish the love that surrounds you, to deepen your connections with others, and to embrace the transformative power of love in all its forms. Love is the force that binds us together as humanity, and in its exploration, we find a deeper understanding of what it means to be human.

Introduction

Love, the ever-pervasive force that courses through the veins of human existence, holds within it the extraordinary power to transform. It is the salve for our wounds, the spark that ignites our dreams, and the invisible thread that weaves us into the intricate tapestry of human connection. In the annals of human experience, love stands as a beacon of hope, a force capable of transmuting the ordinary into the extraordinary.

The meaning of love is a complex and deeply philosophical topic that has been explored and debated by scholars, poets, philosophers, and thinkers throughout history. Love is a multifaceted and profoundly personal experience, and its meaning can vary from person to person and culture to culture. Here are some key aspects of the meaning of love:

1. Emotion and Feeling: Love is often described as a powerful and positive emotion or feeling. It can encompass a wide range of emotions, including affection, care, warmth, attraction, and attachment. Love can bring joy, happiness, and fulfillment to individuals' lives.

2. Connection and Bond: Love is often associated with the idea of forming strong connections and bonds with others. It can involve a deep sense of closeness, intimacy, and connection between individuals, whether in romantic relationships, familial relationships, friendships, or even love for humanity as a whole.

3. Selflessness: Many philosophical and spiritual traditions emphasize the selfless nature of love. It involves caring for and prioritizing the well-being of others, often at the expense of one's own desires or needs. This aspect of love is often associated with compassion and altruism.

4. Commitment: Love can involve a commitment to someone or something. In romantic relationships, this often takes the form of commitment and devotion to a partner. In broader contexts, love can also involve a commitment to a cause, a community, or a set of values.

5. Desire and Attraction: Love can include a strong desire for someone or something. Romantic love, in particular, often involves feelings of passion and intense attraction. This aspect of love is characterized by physical and emotional longing.

6. Unconditional Love: Unconditional love is often seen as the purest form of love, where love is given without any conditions or expectations in return. It is often associated with the love parents have for their children.

7. Spiritual and Transcendent Love: In many spiritual and religious traditions, love takes on a transcendent and divine quality. It is seen as a force that connects individuals to something greater than themselves, whether it's a higher power, the universe, or the collective consciousness of humanity.

8. Complexity and Paradox: Love is often described as both simple and complex, and it can involve paradoxical feelings and experiences. For example, love can bring both joy and pain, it can be both fleeting and enduring, and it can be both liberating and binding.

The metaphor of alchemy, an ancient practice seeking to transmute base metals into gold or to discover the elixir of life, bears a striking resemblance to the transformative nature of love. Alchemists, in their esoteric pursuits, recognized the latent potential within all aspects of nature, awaiting revelation through the careful application of the right elements and rituals. Beyond the physical transmutation, alchemy was viewed as a spiritual odyssey—a path to enlightenment and a harmonious union with the divine.

Much like the alchemist's quest, love, too, can be regarded as a vehicle for personal and relational metamorphosis. It serves as the catalyst that guides us towards the discovery of our true selves, hidden talents, and deepest passions. Love empowers us to confront our fears, transcend limitations, and mend the rifts that divide us. It is the force that elevates human connection beyond the mundane and ushers it into the realm of the extraordinary.

Throughout this exploration, we shall embark on a journey to unravel the concept of love as a transformative force. We will witness its ability to reshape our perception of reality, redefine our sense of self, influence our relationships with others, and forge connections with the universe.

Moreover, we will delve into the everyday occurrences where love manifests its extraordinary nature—whether it be in art, music, literature, or the natural world. These instances will illuminate how love, in its myriad forms, enriches our lives, adorning them with unparalleled beauty, boundless joy, and a profound sense of wonder. As we venture forth, we shall uncover the extraordinary within the ordinary, and in doing so, unveil the remarkable essence of love.

It's important to recognize that the meaning of love can evolve and change over time and can be deeply personal. Different cultures, belief systems, and individuals may have their own interpretations and experiences of love. Ultimately, the meaning of love is a profound and subjective aspect of the human experience that continues to be explored and celebrated in various forms of art, literature, and philosophy.

"The Alchemy of Love: Turning the Ordinary into the Extraordinary" is a book that delves into the profound and transformative nature of love, showing how it has the power to elevate the everyday moments of our lives into something truly extraordinary.

Chapter 1

The Hidden Magic of Love

What is love? This is a question that has puzzled and fascinated humans for centuries. Love is often described as a feeling, an emotion, a state of mind, or a force of nature. But love is more than that. Love is a hidden magic that can transform our lives in ways we cannot imagine.

Love can heal us from our pain and suffering. Love can inspire us to pursue our dreams and passions. Love can connect us with others who share our values and vision. Love can also transform us into better versions of ourselves, by helping us grow, learn, and evolve.

Love is not something that we find or receive from others. Love is something that we create and give to ourselves and others. Love is an act of will, a choice, a commitment, and a practice. Love is also a gift, a blessing, a miracle, and a mystery.

Love, a multifaceted and intricate emotion, defies simple classification. Two notable approaches to understanding and categorizing the types of love have emerged—one rooted in ancient Greek philosophy and another based on modern concepts known as the "five love languages." Let's delve into both perspectives:

Ancient Greek Philosophy: The Eight Types of Love

The wisdom of ancient Greek philosophy offers a nuanced perspective, classifying love into eight distinct types, each defined by a unique blend of three fundamental components: intimacy, passion, and commitment.

1. Agape: This is the embodiment of unconditional, selfless, and spiritual love. Often associated with altruism and divine affection, it transcends personal desires.

2. Eros: A passionate, romantic, and physical love, Eros is ignited by intense sexual attraction and desire. It kindles the flames of passionate romance.

3. Philia: Rooted in deep affection, platonic bonds, and friendship, Philia thrives on mutual respect and shared values. It symbolizes the warmth of genuine camaraderie.

4. Storge: Characterized by familial love, Storge embodies protective and nurturing sentiments. It is the natural, unbreakable bond between parents and children or among siblings.

5. Ludus: Love takes on a playful, flirtatious, and casual form with Ludus. It is an expression of care marked by fun, excitement, and a lower level of commitment.

6. Pragma: Practical, rational, and enduring, Pragma love is grounded in common goals, compatibility, and shared long-term interests. It thrives on pragmatic considerations.

7. Philautia: Self-love, self-esteem, and self-compassion are at the core of Philautia. Depending on its balance, it can be either healthy or unhealthy, impacting one's overall well-being.

8. Mania: Mania manifests as an obsessive, possessive, and dependent form of love. Fueled by insecurity, jealousy, and low self-worth, it often leads to tumultuous relationships.

Modern Concept: The Five Love Languages by Gary Chapman

A contemporary perspective on love centers around the concept of the "five love languages," as defined by Gary Chapman. These languages represent diverse ways that people express and receive love:

1. Words of Affirmation: Love is conveyed through verbal expressions of praise, compliments, and appreciation, reinforcing the power of positive words.

2. Acts of Service: Love is demonstrated by performing helpful deeds and acts of service for the other person, such as chores, favors, or meaningful tasks.

3. Receiving Gifts: Tangible symbols of affection, like flowers, cards, or jewelry, are the means through which love is communicated and received.

4. Quality Time: Love is expressed through the gift of undivided attention and meaningful moments spent together, strengthening emotional bonds.

5. Physical Touch: Physical contact, encompassing hugs, kisses, or cuddles, becomes the language of love, conveying intimacy and affection.

Understanding these diverse approaches to love not only deepens self-awareness but also enriches relationships by fostering effective communication and heightened relationship satisfaction. Love, in all its forms and expressions, continues to be a boundless and fascinating human experience.

In this chapter, we will explore the hidden magic of love in different dimensions of our lives. We will see how love can change our perception of reality, our sense of identity, our attitude towards others, and our connection with the universe. We will also look at some examples of how love manifests itself in everyday situations, such as in art, music, literature, and nature. We will discover how love can enrich our lives with beauty, joy, and wonder.

The Mystery of Love

In the quiet corners of our hearts and the unassuming moments of our lives, there exists a hidden magic—a force that can turn the ordinary into the extraordinary. This magic, as ancient as humanity itself, is love. Welcome to the journey of discovering the enchantment and alchemy of love, where we will explore how this extraordinary force permeates the fabric of our existence.

"The Mystery of Love," a haunting melody penned by Sufjan Stevens, made its debut on the soundtrack of the 2017 cinematic masterpiece, "Call Me By Your Name." This soul-stirring composition earned itself a prestigious nomination for the Academy Award for Best Original Song. Its lyrical narrative delves deep into the labyrinthine realms of love, weaving a tapestry that entwines themes of love's allure, the ache of loss, and the poignant pang of longing.

In its lyrical voyage, "The Mystery of Love" also tips its hat to historical and mythological luminaries, casting a spotlight on figures like Alexander the Great and his beloved Hephaestion. The song pays homage to the M.A.N. (Museo Archeologico Nazionale of Naples), an evocative setting where certain scenes from the film unfolded.

Yet, "The Mystery of Love" is not confined to the realms of cinema or music; it transcends the boundaries of artistry. This enigmatic theme has been an enduring muse for philosophers, poets, and artists across the ages. Their collective endeavors have sought to define, classify, and fathom the diverse facets and manifestations of love.

The ancient Greeks, in their wisdom, parsed love into eight distinct varieties, forged by the interplay of intimacy, passion, and commitment. These multifaceted expressions of love continue to intrigue and captivate us.

For some, love is a deeply emotional and spiritual journey—a union with the divine that mystics have ardently pursued. Others, like the romantics, have exalted love as the wellspring of inspiration and the embodiment of beauty.

Yet, the "Mystery of Love" remains a uniquely personal odyssey, traversed differently by each individual. Love may come effortlessly to some, a natural and harmonious melody, while for others, it may be a tumultuous and arduous symphony. Expressions of love are as varied as the hues of a painter's palette—spoken words, heartfelt deeds, thoughtful gifts, shared moments, or tender touches.

Some may find solace in the embrace of one cherished soul, while others embrace a tapestry of affections, embracing multiple loves simultaneously. Love can manifest as an enduring and steadfast sentinel or as a fleeting and ephemeral wisp of emotion.

Indeed, "The Mystery of Love" is an intricate and endlessly fascinating narrative that awakens our curiosity, ignites our wonder, and kindles the flames of creativity. It remains a timeless enigma, an evergreen source of exploration, inspiration, and profound human connection.

Love has captivated the human imagination for as long as we can remember. It's a force that defies easy definition, for it encompasses a spectrum of emotions, from tenderness and affection to desire and passion. Love is both the gentle whisper of a mother to her child and the fiery ardor between lovers. It's the hand that reaches out in friendship and the selfless act of kindness to a stranger. Love is the emotional canvas upon which we paint the rich tapestry of our lives.

Yet, for all its ubiquity and centrality to our human experience, love remains a mystery. It cannot be fully grasped or contained within the confines of words or theories. Love, like the deepest ocean or the vastness of the cosmos, eludes our attempts to confine it to the rational boundaries of our understanding. It is, in its essence, a profound and beautiful enigma.

Love's Transformative Power

What makes love truly remarkable is its transformative power. It possesses the ability to take the ordinary and infuse it with the extraordinary. It turns mundane moments into cherished memories, and it bestows meaning upon the simplest of actions. Love's magic lies not in grand gestures alone but also in the small, everyday acts of kindness, empathy, and connection.

Embracing the Essence of Love's Transformation beckons you to unfurl the petals of your heart and bask in the inexhaustible richness of existence. Love stands as an indomitable force, intricately weaving the threads of your life into the vast tapestry of the world. While it finds its roots in the deeply personal, love transcends the boundaries of the self, drawing you into the intricate embrace of the human family and the vast ecosystem of life.

Indeed, love is an emotion, coursing through the chambers of your heart with profound intensity. Yet, it is also a resounding call to action, a summons to participate actively in the world around you. In its essence, love ignites a spark within you, propelling you towards the profound interconnection that binds all living beings and inviting you to partake in the symphony of life's great dance.

Consider the way a shared smile between strangers can brighten both their days, and how a lovingly prepared meal can nourish not just the body but also the soul. Love has the power to mend broken hearts, bridge divides, and inspire acts of heroism. It transforms us, molding us into better versions of ourselves, and it has the capacity to heal wounds—both physical and emotional.

A Journey Through History: Love Across the Epochs

Love is a universal mystery that has fascinated humans throughout time and space. As we travel across the historical epochs, we encounter different ways of understanding and expressing this complex and dynamic force.

Different thinkers have offered different perspectives on love. Waldo Tobler's idea that "love is related to everything else, but near things are more related than distant things" suggests that love creates a network of connections among all things. However, despite our intuitive insights and the profound wisdom of thinkers like Tobler, we still cannot capture the full essence of love in a single definition.

Empedocles and Strife: Ancient Echoes

In the ancient world, we meet Empedocles, a pre-Socratic philosopher who proposed that Love (Philotes) and Strife (Neikos) were the two fundamental forces of the universe. Love, in his vision, was a unifying force that sought to overcome the separation of all things. Strife, on the contrary, was a divisive force that introduced disorder and conflict. In this ancient cosmology, love was a primal cosmic principle.

Plato's Eros and Aristotle's Philia: Socratic Contemplations

The classical era brought forth the philosophical reflections of Socrates, Plato, and Aristotle on the nature of love. Plato, in his symposium, presented Eros—a love that transcended the physical world, a longing for the eternal and the beautiful. Aristotle, on the other hand, explored Philia—a love based on friendship and mutual respect, a lasting bond that enriched human relationships.

St. Paul's Agape and St. Augustine's Caritas: Medieval Reverie

In the medieval times, St. Paul introduced the concept of Agape—a divine, selfless love that connected humanity to God and to each other. St. Augustine elaborated on this idea with Caritas, emphasizing the transformative power of love as a guiding force in the human soul. Love, for these theologians, was a powerful agent of change, capable of elevating the human spirit.

Rousseau's Emile and Sophie: Renaissance Romance

As the Renaissance emerged, Jean-Jacques Rousseau created a modern vision of love with his characters Emile and Sophie. In this romantic story, love became the catalyst for personal growth and the foundation of an idealized partnership. Rousseau's perspective on love highlighted the evolving nature of human relationships.

Freud's Transference: Modern Explorations

The modern era ushered in a new understanding of love through the lens of Sigmund Freud. His analysis of love as transference revealed the intricate dynamics of the human psyche. Love, in Freud's view, often appeared as a projection of our inner desires and conflicts onto others, unraveling the complexities of human emotion.

Navigating the Bonds to Children: Postmodern Duties

In the postmodern world, we face the notion of love as a duty, especially in relation to parental love. This contemporary exploration examines the responsibilities and ethical considerations involved in nurturing and guiding the next generation. Love, it seems, takes on multifaceted roles in our changing world.

A Tapestry of Love: Interwoven Threads

Throughout this journey, we realize that these concepts of love are not isolated from each other. Rather, they form an intricate tapestry, with later philosophers often building upon the foundations laid by their predecessors. Love, in its diverse manifestations, remains an enduring force, shaping human existence and offering a window into the evolving nature of our collective consciousness.

Stories of Love's Magic

Throughout this journey, we will encounter stories and experiences that illustrate love's hidden magic. We will delve into the lives of individuals who have witnessed love's extraordinary power firsthand—stories of love's ability to heal, inspire, and transform. These narratives will serve as beacons, guiding us through the intricate labyrinth of love's mysteries.

But beyond the stories, we will also explore the science and psychology behind love, seeking to understand the mechanisms that underlie its magic. We will uncover the profound impact love has on our well-being, relationships, and the world around us.

As we embark on this exploration, open your heart to the possibility that love is not just an emotion but a potent force that can elevate every facet of your life. Prepare to be amazed by the hidden magic of love, and let us journey together into the depths of this extraordinary force that has the power to turn the ordinary into something truly extraordinary.

Chapter 2

The Alchemical Elements of Love

Love is not a monolithic entity; rather, it is a complex interplay of elements that come together to create a profound and transformative experience. In this chapter, we will dissect the alchemy of love, breaking it down into its essential components. Just as a skilled alchemist blends different elements to create something precious, so too does love draw from various emotional and psychological components to work its magic.

The Elements of Love

Harmonizing Love: The Alchemical Dance of the Four Elements

In the intricate tapestry of human emotions, love stands as a force of unparalleled magnitude. To unravel its mysteries and grasp its essence, we embark on a journey that invokes the wisdom of the ages—the alchemical elements of air, water, fire, and earth. These elemental building blocks, when applied to the realm of love, reveal profound insights into the multifaceted nature of this extraordinary force.

Air: The Breath of Commitment

In the realm of love, commitment is the air we breathe—a vital element that sustains the bonds we forge. Much like the gentle caress of a breeze, commitment offers a sense of security, a promise to stand unwaveringly by one another's side. It is the whispered vows of devotion, the unspoken pledge to weather life's storms together. Just as air fills our lungs, commitment infuses our relationships with life, enabling them to flourish and endure.

Water: The Flow of Connection

Love, like water, flows through the channels of human connection. It is the gentle stream that carves its path through the landscape of our hearts, forging profound bonds of empathy, understanding, and intimacy. Love's waters run deep, nourishing the roots of our relationships and allowing them to grow stronger with time. It is the tears of joy and sorrow, the shared laughter, and the profound moments of vulnerability that shape the fluidity of love's connection.

Fire: The Chemistry of Passion

In the crucible of love, passion burns like a raging fire—an elemental force that ignites desire, longing, and intensity. It is the spark that kindles romance, the flame that warms our souls, and the heat that fuels our deepest desires. Love's fire consumes us, drawing us into its fervent embrace and forging unbreakable bonds of attraction and ardor. It is the magnetic pull that binds us together, creating a chemistry that defies explanation.

Earth: The Foundation of Consistency

As love takes root, it finds its foundation in the solid ground of earth—an element that symbolizes consistency, stability, and reliability. Love, like the earth beneath our feet, provides a steady platform upon which we can build our lives. It is the unwavering support, the rock-solid presence, and the steadfast commitment to one another's well-being. Love's earthy embrace offers a sense of security, allowing us to weather life's challenges with resilience and fortitude.

The Alchemical Balance: Nurturing Healthy Love

To cultivate a healthy and harmonious relationship, one must recognize and balance these alchemical elements of love. Like a skilled alchemist, we must tend to the delicate interplay of commitment, connection, chemistry, and consistency. In doing so, we unlock the secrets of enduring love—a love that breathes life into our existence, flows through the depths of our souls, burns with an undying passion, and stands as an unwavering foundation.

Imagine love as a magnificent tapestry woven from threads of passion, compassion, empathy, and commitment. Each of these elements contributes its unique hue and texture, forming a masterpiece that is greater than the sum of its parts. Let's explore these elements in more detail:

1. Passion: Passion ignites the flames of love. It's the intense desire, attraction, and emotional connection that often characterize the early stages of romantic relationships. It's the racing heart, the butterflies in your stomach, and the yearning for closeness. Passion is the element that infuses love with energy and vitality.

2. Compassion: Compassion is the gentle and caring side of love. It involves empathy and a deep concern for the well-being of others. Compassion allows us to understand and share in the joys and sorrows of those we love. It's the comforting hand on a friend's shoulder or the willingness to lend a helping hand to someone in need.

3. Empathy: Empathy is the ability to truly understand and connect with another person's feelings and experiences. It's the capacity to see the world from their perspective and to be present with them in their joys and struggles. Empathy is the bridge that allows us to forge deep emotional connections with others.

4. Commitment: Commitment is the sturdy foundation upon which lasting love is built. It involves a sense of dedication and responsibility to a relationship or a cause. It's the promise to stand by someone through thick and thin, to weather the storms of life together. Commitment is what keeps love steady and enduring.

As we embrace the alchemical elements of love, we embark on a transformative journey—a journey that allows us to navigate the intricate terrain of human emotion with grace and wisdom. In this dance of the elements, we discover the profound beauty and boundless potential of love, reminding us that, like the elements themselves, love is an eternal and elemental force that shapes the very essence of our being.

Nurturing Love's Elements

Understanding these elements of love is just the beginning. To truly harness the power of love's alchemy, we must learn how to nurture and balance these components within ourselves and our relationships. Here are some key insights:

- Balancing Passion and Compassion: While passion adds excitement to love, compassion ensures its gentleness. Finding the equilibrium between these two elements is essential for healthy and enduring relationships.

- Cultivating Empathy: Empathy is a skill that can be developed. By actively listening, seeking to understand others, and practicing kindness, we can enhance our capacity for empathy and deepen our connections.

- Embracing Commitment: Commitment is not just about sticking around; it's about actively choosing to invest in a relationship. It involves communication, compromise, and a willingness to work through challenges together.

As we continue our exploration of love, keep in mind that the magic of love lies in the balance and interplay of these elements. Love's alchemy is not a static process; it evolves and deepens over time. In the chapters that follow, we will delve deeper into each of these elements and discover how they shape the extraordinary nature of love.

Chapter 3

Love's Power to Heal

Love is more than a fleeting emotion or a momentary burst of passion. It possesses a profound and often underestimated power: the ability to heal. In this chapter, we will delve into the ways in which love acts as a balm for our physical and emotional wounds, mending what is broken and nurturing our well-being.

- Love can speed up wound healing by enhancing the immune system and reducing inflammation.
- Love can increase longevity by reducing the risk of premature death and chronic diseases.
- Love can improve mental health by reducing depression, anxiety, and suicide risk.
- Love can enhance spiritual health by connecting us to the divine and our true nature.

The Healing Touch of Love

Think back to a time when love, in its various forms, brought comfort and solace to your life. It could be a mother's kiss on a scraped knee, a friend's comforting words during a difficult time, or the tender care of a partner when you were feeling unwell. These moments are not mere coincidences; they are manifestations of love's innate ability to heal.

Emotional Healing

Embarking on the Path of Emotional Healing: Nurturing Well-Being and Relationships

Emotional healing is a transformative journey—a journey that beckons you to acknowledge, embrace, and navigate the intricate landscape of your emotions. It is a profound process that holds the power to mend wounds, elevate well-being, and fortify the bonds that connect you to others.

At its core, emotional healing begins with the courageous act of acknowledging your emotions. It is an invitation to turn your gaze inward, to confront the myriad feelings that reside within you—both joyous and painful. By recognizing the emotional tapestry that colors your inner world, you embark on a path of self-discovery and self-compassion.

Acceptance is the cornerstone of this healing voyage. It is the gentle embrace of your emotions, without judgment or condemnation. In the tender act of accepting your feelings, you grant yourself permission to be human—to experience the full spectrum of emotions that course through your heart. It is an act of self-love, a testament to your inherent worthiness.

As you traverse this transformative path, you will encounter the essence of processing your emotions—a sacred alchemy that transmutes pain into wisdom, and sorrow into resilience. It is a journey of introspection, a voyage into the depths of your soul, where you explore the origins and meanings of your emotions. Through introspective contemplation and mindful reflection, you unravel the intricate threads of your emotional tapestry.

Emotional healing is not a solitary endeavor; it is a collaborative dance with your inner self. It calls for patience, self-compassion, and self-care. It is the tender act of nurturing your well-being, of tending to your emotional wounds with kindness and grace. As you heal, you emerge stronger, more resilient, and more attuned to the ebb and flow of your emotions.

Yet, the ripple effects of emotional healing extend far beyond the boundaries of your inner world. They reach outwards, enriching the tapestry of your relationships. Emotional healing enhances your capacity for empathy and understanding, fostering deeper connections with those you hold dear. It is a gift you offer not only to yourself but also to those who share in your journey.

In the tapestry of life, emotional healing weaves threads of growth, resilience, and transformation. It is a process that invites you to embrace the fullness of your humanity, to honor the richness of your emotional landscape, and to emerge from the crucible of experience with a heart that is open, compassionate, and resilient.

1. Support in Times of Sorrow: Love provides a shoulder to cry on during our darkest moments. Whether we've experienced loss, heartbreak, or disappointment, the love and support of others can help us navigate the depths of our emotions.

2. Reducing Stress and Anxiety: Love has a calming effect on our minds and bodies. The presence of a loved one, whether human or animal, can lower stress levels and reduce anxiety. The knowledge that we are not alone in our struggles can be incredibly soothing.

3. Boosting Self-Esteem: Unconditional love, especially from parents or caregivers during childhood, plays a significant role in shaping our self-esteem. Feeling loved and accepted for who we are fosters a sense of self-worth that can last a lifetime.

As you embark on this sacred journey of emotional healing, may you find solace in the profound wisdom that lies within your emotions. May you discover the boundless strength that resides in your vulnerability. And may you nurture the well-being of your soul and the depth of your relationships, for emotional healing is a testament to the enduring power of the human spirit to grow, thrive, and flourish.

Physical Healing

Physical Healing: Nurturing the Restoration of Body and Soul

Physical healing is a profound journey—a journey that unfolds in response to the body's plea for restoration, an intricate process that seeks to mend the fragile tapestry of life. When an organism confronts physical trauma or disease, healing becomes the beacon of hope, the promise of renewal, and the resumption of normalcy.

At its core, healing is the intricate orchestration of cellular regeneration—a symphony of life that plays out within the confines of our biological system. It is the miraculous transformation that reduces the scars of damage, replaces the necrotic with vibrant living tissue, and restores the intricate machinery of the body to its harmonious functioning.

The term "physical healing" is versatile, adopting different hues depending on the context in which it resides. In its broadest sense, it signifies the meticulous process of reclaiming health and vitality after the onslaught of injury, illness, or disease. The pursuit of physical healing unfolds through a myriad of methods, encompassing the realms of modern medicine, surgical interventions, therapeutic modalities, and alternative approaches that honor the profound connection between body and soul.

Balancing the Elemental Forces: The Ancient Greek Perspective

One lens through which we can contemplate physical healing draws from the wisdom of ancient Greek philosophy—the four classical elements: air, water, fire, and earth. According to this paradigm, each element embodies a distinct facet of physical healing. Air echoes the commitment to life's breath, water represents the nurturing connection between body and nature, fire embodies the transformative chemistry of the body's processes, and earth symbolizes the unwavering consistency of our bodily functions. By harmonizing and nurturing these elemental forces, we embark on a journey towards a healthy and harmonious relationship with ourselves and others.

Faith and Healing: The Christian Perspective

In the realm of faith, particularly within the Christian tradition, physical healing resonates as a powerful testament to the union of body and soul. It is a belief that prayer, fortified by unwavering faith in the divine, possesses the potential to catalyze the miraculous restoration of health. This faith-infused healing manifests through two principal avenues: intercessory prayer and the laying of hands.

Intercessory prayer, a collective plea for divine intervention, rests on the premise that the earnest supplications of the faithful can move the heart of the divine. In response to these fervent petitions, it is believed that God, in His infinite mercy, may grant healing to the afflicted.

The laying of hands, a sacred act, calls upon certain individuals—recognized as healers—to channel the healing energies of the divine into the body of the ailing. Through the gentle touch of these healers, it is believed that the transformative powers of God are summoned, facilitating the restoration of physical well-being.

In the tapestry of existence, physical healing stands as a testament to the intricate interplay of science and spirituality, of medicine and faith. It is a journey that celebrates the profound resilience of the human body, the boundless potential of the human spirit, and the enduring hope that healing offers.

Physical Healing involves:

1. Enhanced Immunity: Studies have shown that people in loving and supportive relationships tend to have stronger immune systems. Love's positive impact on stress reduction may contribute to this boost in immunity.

2. Faster Recovery: Patients who feel loved and supported often experience faster recoveries from illnesses or surgeries. The emotional strength derived from love can translate into physical resilience.

3. Pain Relief: Love triggers the release of natural painkillers in the body, making us more tolerant of physical discomfort. The comfort of a loved one's touch or presence can alleviate pain.

As we contemplate physical healing, may we honor the intricate dance between body and soul. May we recognize the harmony that emerges when science and faith converge in their quest to restore the fragile balance of life. In the embrace of physical healing, we find solace, renewal, and the enduring promise that the body's capacity for renewal is a testament to the miraculous nature of existence itself.

Love's Role in Longevity

Beyond immediate healing, love plays a pivotal role in our overall health and longevity. People who maintain strong social connections and experience love throughout their lives tend to live longer and healthier lives. The sense of purpose and belonging that love provides contributes to a fulfilling and extended existence.

Love, in its myriad forms, plays a substantial and multifaceted role in promoting longevity and overall well-being. The interconnection between love and longevity is a profound testament to the complex relationship between our emotional and physical health. Here, we explore the various ways in which love contributes to a longer and healthier life.

1. Reducing Stress

Love, particularly in the form of close relationships and social support, serves as a powerful buffer against stress. When individuals feel loved and supported, their bodies release lower levels of stress hormones like cortisol. Chronic stress is linked to a host of health problems, including heart disease, high blood pressure, and weakened immune function. By providing emotional comfort and a sense of security, love can mitigate the detrimental effects of stress, ultimately promoting longevity.

2. Boosting Immunity

Positive emotions associated with love, such as happiness and contentment, have been linked to enhanced immune function. When individuals experience love, their bodies release feel-good neurotransmitters like dopamine and endorphins, which, in turn, can bolster the immune system. A robust immune system is better equipped to defend against infections and chronic diseases, contributing to a longer and healthier life.

3. Promoting Healthy Behaviors

Love often encourages individuals to adopt healthier lifestyles. In nurturing relationships, couples may support each other in making positive choices, such as eating well, exercising regularly, and avoiding harmful behaviors like smoking or excessive alcohol consumption. These health-conscious behaviors can have a significant impact on longevity by reducing the risk of chronic diseases.

4. Enhancing Mental Health

Love's profound emotional support can greatly contribute to mental well-being. Strong, loving relationships provide a sense of purpose, belonging, and emotional security, which are essential for maintaining good mental health. Individuals in loving relationships are less likely to experience depression, anxiety, and loneliness, all of which can take a toll on one's overall health and longevity.

5. Strengthening Resilience

Love fosters resilience in the face of life's challenges. When individuals have a support system of loved ones, they are better equipped to navigate difficult circumstances, cope with loss, and adapt to change. This emotional resilience can help mitigate the negative health effects of chronic stress and adversity, ultimately promoting a longer and more fulfilling life.

6. Reducing Risk of Cardiovascular Disease

Studies have shown that individuals in loving relationships tend to have lower rates of heart disease and improved cardiovascular health. Love's positive impact on stress reduction, emotional well-being, and healthy behaviors contributes to a healthier heart and a reduced risk of heart-related ailments.

7. Increasing Longevity

Numerous studies have linked love and longevity. Whether through marriage, close friendships, or strong familial bonds, people in loving relationships tend to live longer lives. The emotional, psychological, and physical benefits of love collectively contribute to a greater likelihood of reaching old age in good health.

In summary, love's role in promoting longevity is both profound and multifaceted. It reduces stress, boosts immunity, encourages healthy behaviors, enhances mental health, strengthens resilience, reduces the risk of cardiovascular disease, and increases overall life expectancy. The power of love extends beyond the heart and soul—it touches every aspect of our being, contributing to a longer and more fulfilling life.

The Healing Act of Giving Love

The Art and Science of Giving

From our earliest days, we're instilled with the wisdom that giving is a virtue surpassing the act of receiving. The altruistic act of giving, a cornerstone of humanity's moral compass, brings a sense of fulfillment as we aid those in need. But beneath the surface of this timeless wisdom lies a profound undercurrent—an inquiry into the deeper significance of giving.

"If you want happiness for an hour, take a nap. If you want happiness for a day, go fishing. If you want happiness for a year, inherit a fortune. If you want happiness for a lifetime, help somebody," imparts an ancient Chinese proverb, offering a glimpse into the transcendent power of giving.

While philosophers and saints have extolled the virtues of giving, the realm of science and empirical data also echoes a resounding affirmation—giving is indeed as beneficial for the giver as it is for the recipient.

In the annals of contemporary research, compelling evidence emerges to underscore the notion that sharing one's time, talents, and treasures serves as a transformative path to discovering purpose, transcending personal trials, and unearthing profound fulfillment and meaning in life.

Survival of the Kindest

Within the hallowed halls of the University of California, Berkeley, a paradigm shift challenges age-old convictions that humans are inherently driven by selfish inclinations. A growing body of scientific inquiry suggests that we, as a species, are undergoing an evolution towards greater compassion and collaboration—a transformation aimed at ensuring our survival and flourishing.

Dacher Keltner, co-director of UC Berkeley's Greater Good Science Center, sheds light on this evolutionary shift, stating, "Because of our very vulnerable offspring, the fundamental task for human survival and gene replication is to take care of others. Human beings have survived as a species because we have evolved the capacities to care for those in need and to cooperate."

Does this stance contradict Charles Darwin's enduring principle of "survival of the fittest," where self-preservation takes precedence? The answer, it appears, is a resounding no. In his work, "The Descent of Man," Darwin himself invokes the concept of benevolence 99 times, culminating in the recognition that love, sympathy, and cooperation are intrinsic to the natural world. Just as a pelican may provide sustenance to a blind member of its flock, empathy and cooperation are woven into the fabric of existence.

"As Darwin long ago surmised, sympathy is our strongest instinct," Keltner concludes, bridging the worlds of science and altruism.

It's essential to recognize that love's healing power is not unidirectional. While we receive healing from the love of others, we also have the capacity to heal through the act of giving love. Offering compassion, support, and care to those in need not only improves their well-being but also nurtures our own.

Conclusion

Love's power to heal is both profound and far-reaching. Whether it's healing emotional wounds, bolstering our physical well-being, or contributing to a longer and more fulfilling life, love's ability to mend is a testament to its extraordinary nature. As we move forward in this exploration, we will continue to uncover the multifaceted ways in which love touches our lives, enriching our experiences and making us whole.

Chapter 4

Love and Transformation

Love is a catalyst for change, a force that has the remarkable ability to transform individuals and relationships. In this chapter, we will explore the profound transformations that love can bring about in our lives and the ways in which it shapes our personal growth and self-discovery.

Genuine Love Unveiled

Genuine love is a deliberate attitude and unwavering commitment to the personal growth and well-being of oneself and another. It's a profound intimacy that only materializes when one confronts their fears, addresses their inner struggles, and comes to a deep understanding and love for their own self. This love manifests as an unfiltered expression of one's true self, absent any expectations for others to conform or change. It doesn't imply perpetual peace and harmony where the dishes and laundry are eternally spotless. Instead, it's a commitment to the growth and well-being of another, a journey marked by conflicts, negotiations, and self-discovery within the tapestry of everyday life. It's in the minutiae that the divine resides.

Genuine love is an act of will and dedication. Erich Fromm, in his wisdom, postulates that falling in love is, fundamentally, a conscious choice—an act of will. It's a decision, a judgment, he contends, shaped not by the other person but by the workings of one's mind. Furthermore, he asserts that concentrating all one's love on a single individual isn't genuine love; it's a 'symbiotic attachment' or an enlarged ego. Fromm suggests that this stems from the need for security or validation of self-worth.

How Our Perceptions of Love Become Distorted

Our perceptions of love often become distorted from an early age. The foundation of what we perceive as love, the lessons we learn about it, often stem from our parents' needs and fears. While this may appear as a general statement, research substantiates this claim.

Psychologist and author Alice Miller, in her work 'For Your Own Good,' argues that parents, unable to differentiate their own needs from a genuine expression of love for their children, manipulate and coerce their offspring into costumes of their design—costumes they would be pleased to see their children wear. These costumes, however, may not align with their children's true desires or comfort. Children, yearning for their parents' love and a sense of self-worth, contort themselves to fit into these costumes, even though they inherently know they don't fit.

This scenario parallels someone loving you solely because you shop at the 'right' stores—it's not love for who you are, but for the facade you present. Parents, although unaware of their actions, unintentionally perpetuate this cycle. They want to love their children, but the inability to distinguish between their needs and genuine love results in unintentional harm.

Daniel Hughes, a psychologist, identifies the essential elements that children require from parents to mature into emotionally stable adults who remain true to themselves—P.L.A.C.E:

P - Play
L - Love
A - Acceptance
C - Curiosity
E - Empathy

Without these elements, children often construct a false self—a mask—to conceal their perceived flaws and unworthiness. Consequently, many of us wear these masks dutifully, occasionally becoming aware of their constrictive nature and attempting to shed them. Yet, discarding these masks exposes us, leaving us feeling vulnerable and ashamed. We mistakenly believe that the mask is what earns us love, and without it, we deem ourselves worthless.

The Power of Love to Transform

The Transformative Power of Love

Love possesses an extraordinary capacity to instigate profound transformations in our lives. It is a force that can shape and reshape our existence, guiding us towards growth, healing, and self-realization. Here, we delve into the remarkable ways in which the power of love can catalyze profound personal and societal changes.

1. Self-Discovery and Acceptance

Love serves as a mirror, reflecting our true selves with unwavering honesty. When we experience love—be it through self-love or in the context of a loving relationship—it compels us to explore the depths of our identity. We confront our fears, insecurities, and past wounds, gradually learning to accept and embrace every facet of our being. Love encourages us to shed the masks we wear and reveals the authenticity that lies beneath.

2. Healing and Wholeness

Love possesses a remarkable capacity to heal emotional wounds and scars that have lingered within us for years. It acts as a soothing balm, mending the fractures in our hearts and souls. Through the nurturing power of love, we find solace, resilience, and the strength to confront past traumas. It is in the embrace of love that we discover the transformative potential of forgiveness, both for ourselves and others.

3. Empathy and Connection

Love fosters a profound sense of empathy and connection with the world around us. It encourages us to step into the shoes of others, to understand their struggles, hopes, and dreams. This empathetic connection extends beyond our immediate relationships, inspiring us to extend our compassion and support to all living beings. In this way, love has the power to dissolve boundaries and promote unity on a global scale.

4. Growth and Personal Development

Love is an ever-evolving force that propels us toward personal growth and development. It encourages us to set aside our comfort zones and embark on journeys of self-improvement. Through love, we find the motivation to pursue our passions, hone our talents, and strive for excellence. Love compels us to become the best versions of ourselves, not only for our sake but for the enrichment of those we hold dear.

5. Social Change and Compassion

The power of love extends beyond individual transformation; it has the potential to catalyze societal change. When communities and societies prioritize love as a guiding principle, compassion, and empathy become driving forces. Acts of kindness, social justice, and collective well-being take precedence. Love fuels movements that seek to eradicate injustice, discrimination, and inequality, creating a more just and compassionate world.

6. Resilience in Adversity

In times of adversity and hardship, love provides a vital source of resilience. It bolsters our ability to navigate challenges, offering emotional sustenance and a sense of purpose. Love empowers us to weather life's storms with unwavering determination, emerging from difficulties stronger and more compassionate than before.

7. Inspiration and Creativity

Love has long been celebrated as a wellspring of inspiration and creativity. It ignites our imagination, fueling artistic expression and innovation. Countless works of art, literature, music, and scientific discoveries have been inspired by the profound emotions that love evokes. It is through love that we tap into our creative potential, producing works that transcend time and resonate with the human spirit.

In conclusion, the transformative power of love is a potent force that shapes our individual journeys and the course of human history. It propels us towards self-discovery, healing, empathy, personal growth, social change, resilience, and creative expression. Love, in all its forms, is the catalyst for the profound transformations that make life rich and meaningful.

Imagine a caterpillar undergoing metamorphosis to become a butterfly. Love has a similar transformative power, often taking us from one state of being to another, revealing our true selves, and helping us grow and evolve.

1. Self-Discovery through Love

One of the most transformative aspects of love is its capacity to help us discover who we truly are. When we love and are loved in return, we often gain deeper insights into our values, desires, and aspirations. Love provides a mirror in which we see ourselves more clearly, allowing us to recognize our strengths, weaknesses, and potential for growth.

2. Personal Growth

Love challenges us to become better versions of ourselves. It encourages us to overcome our fears, insecurities, and limitations. Whether it's a romantic relationship, a familial bond, or a deep friendship, love often calls us to rise above our own expectations and become more compassionate, patient, and understanding individuals.

3. Expanding Empathy

Empathy, a vital element of love, expands our capacity to understand and connect with others on a deeper level. As we love and are loved, we become more attuned to the emotions and experiences of those around us. This heightened empathy not only strengthens our relationships but also makes us more compassionate and considerate members of society.

4. The Transformation of Relationships

Love doesn't just transform individuals; it also shapes the dynamics of our relationships. Healthy love relationships evolve over time, growing deeper and more resilient. They navigate challenges, adapt to changing circumstances, and continue to provide sources of support, comfort, and joy.

Case Studies in Transformation

Throughout this chapter, we will explore case studies and real-life examples of individuals whose lives were profoundly transformed by love. These stories illustrate the remarkable capacity of love to bring about change, often in unexpected and awe-inspiring ways.

The Role of Self-Love

While much of this chapter focuses on the transformative power of love in the context of relationships with others, it's important to emphasize the role of self-love. Self-love is the foundation upon which all other forms of love are built. When we love ourselves, we are better equipped to love and be loved by others. Self-love is the catalyst for personal growth and transformation.

Conclusion

Love is not static; it is a dynamic and evolving force that shapes our lives and helps us grow into the best versions of ourselves. As we continue our journey into the extraordinary nature of love, remember that it is not just a destination but also a path of continuous self-discovery, personal growth, and transformation. Love invites us to embrace change and become the beautiful butterflies of our own unique journeys.

Chapter 5

Love in Different Forms

Love is a multifaceted gem, with each facet representing a different form of affection and connection. In this chapter, we will explore the various manifestations of love, from romantic love to familial love, platonic love, and the profound concept of self-love. Each form of love has its unique qualities and challenges, but they all share the common thread of enriching our lives and deepening our connections with others.

1. Romantic Love

Romantic love is often the first image that comes to mind when we think of love. It's the passionate, exhilarating, and sometimes tumultuous love that exists between partners in a romantic relationship. This form of love is characterized by attraction, desire, and a deep emotional connection. We'll explore the intensity and enchantment of romantic love, as well as the challenges it may pose.

Romantic Love: The Fusion of Passion, Intimacy, and Commitment

Romantic love is a multifaceted emotional experience that intertwines passion, intimacy, and commitment, creating a profound connection between individuals.

1. Passion: At the heart of romantic love lies an intense and irresistible attraction, a fervent desire that sweeps us off our feet. It's the butterflies in your stomach, the racing heart, and the longing for the presence of that special someone. Passion fuels the fires of romance, infusing it with excitement and fervor.

2. Intimacy: Beyond the flames of passion, romantic love thrives on closeness and connection. Intimacy is the profound emotional bond that forms between two individuals. It's the shared secrets, the deep conversations, and the vulnerability that you entrust to your partner. Intimacy nurtures understanding, empathy, and a sense of being truly known.

3. Commitment: In the realm of romantic love, commitment represents the conscious decision to stand by your partner's side through thick and thin. It's the unwavering support, the promise of a shared future, and the dedication to weather life's storms together. Commitment is the bedrock of enduring love, grounding it in a long-term partnership.

The Power and Complexity of Romantic Love

Romantic love is often hailed as one of the most potent and rewarding human emotions. It possesses the power to spark creativity, kindle happiness, and fulfill our deepest longings. This profound emotion serves as a driving force, motivating individuals to surmount challenges, embark on personal growth journeys, and contribute positively to society.

Throughout history, romantic love has been a wellspring of inspiration, serving as the muse for countless artistic and cultural expressions. It has found its voice in poetry, melodies, literary masterpieces, and cinematic tales, capturing the essence of human connection and desire.

Yet, the path of romantic love is not always smooth. It can be fraught with confusion, conflict, and moments of heartache. This complex emotion is susceptible to change, evolving over time due to circumstances, personal growth, and the dynamics between partners. It can either fade like a fleeting star or transform into a deeper, more enduring connection.

Romantic love is also deeply influenced by a tapestry of factors, including individual personality, cultural context, biological predispositions, and personal history. Its intricate dance is shaped by the unique blend of elements that each individual brings to the relationship.

In essence, romantic love is a profound journey marked by passion, intimacy, and commitment—a journey that can inspire, challenge, and ultimately enrich our lives.

2. Familial Love

Familial love encompasses the bonds between family members, including parents and children, siblings, and extended family. This form of love is often marked by a sense of duty, unconditional support, and a shared history. We'll delve into the complexities of family dynamics, the joys of close-knit bonds, and the unique challenges that can arise within family relationships.

Familial Love: The Unconditional Bond

Familial love is an enduring and unique form of affection that finds its expression within the realm of family connections. Whether forged through biological ties, adoption, chosen families, or external bonds, this love transcends boundaries.

In the wisdom of ancient Greek scholars, familial love was known as "storge"—a love that embodies an unconditional and familial essence. What sets storge apart, especially in the context of younger children, is its propensity to be unilateral or asymmetrical, flowing more abundantly from one direction.

On a broader scale, storge encapsulates the warm affection that blossoms from familiarity or interdependence. It's the love that thrives within the cozy embrace of family, rooted in shared experiences, support, and the comforting sense of belonging.

Family: Bound by More Than Blood

Family transcends the confines of mere blood ties. Familial love ushers in a unique realm of emotions, behaviors, challenges, and rewards. In its essence, family represents a collective of individuals who share a common ancestry. However, the beauty of family lies in the ability to form these bonds by choice, irrespective of genetic connections.

Family is a tapestry woven not only from the threads of shared DNA but also from the threads of shared experiences, mutual support, and a deep sense of belonging. It is a sanctuary where love knows no boundaries, where relationships are nurtured, and where the bonds of kinship extend far beyond genetics.

3. Platonic Love

Platonic love is the deep affection and connection we share with our friends and companions. It's the love that exists without romantic or sexual attraction but is characterized by trust, loyalty, and emotional intimacy. We'll explore the beauty of platonic friendships, the enduring nature of these bonds, and the vital role they play in our lives.

Platonic Love: The Pinnacle of Pure Connection

Platonic love, rooted in the philosophy of ancient Greek thinker Plato, is a profound and unique form of affection that transcends the realms of romance and physical desire. Named after Plato, who delved into various facets of love in his dialogue, the Symposium, this love seeks the eternal and the beautiful, striving for a connection that goes beyond the mundane.

In the essence of platonic love lies a depth of friendship and connection that is characterized by mutual respect and shared values. It stands as a testament to the human capacity to form relationships that are untethered to physical attraction or desire. Instead, it is founded on the pillars of profound companionship and a quest for the divine.

Platonic love distinguishes itself from other forms of affection, such as eros (romantic love), philia (friendship love), storge (familial love), ludus (playful love), pragma (practical love), philautia (self-love), and mania (obsessive love). It is often regarded as one of the loftiest and purest expressions of love.

This extraordinary form of love knows no bounds in terms of gender or number of participants. It extends its embrace to both opposite-sex and same-sex relationships, allowing for deep connections to flourish among individuals. Platonic love offers a myriad of advantages, including increased confidence and self-esteem, refined conflict resolution skills, improved mental and spiritual well-being.

Yet, like all forms of love, platonic love carries its own set of challenges and potential pitfalls. Misunderstandings may arise as some may expect or desire more than friendship, leading to unrealistic expectations. It may also spark jealousy or resentment in others and occasionally impede personal growth by fostering dependency.

In its complexity and wonder, platonic love remains a subject that continues to inspire curiosity and exploration, unveiling the profound depths of human connection beyond the confines of physical desire.

4. Self-Love

Self-love is a fundamental form of love that often forms the foundation for all other types of love. It involves treating oneself with kindness, acceptance, and compassion. We'll discuss the importance of self-love for mental and emotional well-being, as well as practical ways to cultivate self-love and self-care in our daily lives.

Embracing Self-Love: Nurturing the Inner You

Self-love is a profound practice rooted in the art of cherishing oneself, safeguarding personal well-being, and cultivating inner happiness. It signifies a deep acceptance of your own being, treating yourself with unwavering kindness, and nurturing your growth and contentment. Beyond this, it encompasses the thoughts and feelings you harbor about your own self, cultivating a positive and authentic self-image.

At its core, self-love forms the bedrock of your relationship with both yourself and the world at large. It propels you towards making choices that honor your physical and emotional health, empowers you to establish boundaries, communicate your needs, and chase your aspirations. It equips you with the resilience to face life's challenges, combat stress, and extend forgiveness, both to yourself and others. The ripple effects of self-love encompass heightened confidence, self-esteem, optimism, and an unwavering capacity to bounce back from adversity.

It is essential to distinguish self-love from narcissism and selfishness. Narcissism, a personality disorder, hinges on an inflated sense of self-importance, a deficiency of empathy, and an insatiable craving for admiration. Selfishness, on the other hand, is a behavior defined by prioritizing personal interests above all else, irrespective of the consequences. In contrast, self-love represents a harmonious and wholesome attitude that respects both the self and others.

The practice of self-love takes on multifaceted forms, including:

- Affirming positive self-talk
- Extending forgiveness for your mistakes
- Fulfilling your own needs
- Asserting yourself
- Safeguarding against exploitation and abuse
- Prioritizing your physical and emotional health
- Surrounding yourself with supportive individuals who uplift and inspire
- Seeking assistance when necessary
- Releasing grudges and resentments that shackle your progress
- Recognizing your unique strengths
- Validating your emotions
- Consistently making healthy choices
- Aligning your actions with your core values
- Pursuing your passions and ambitions
- Challenging yourself to grow
- Holding yourself accountable for your actions
- Indulging in wholesome self-treats
- Embracing your imperfections
- Setting attainable expectations
- Acknowledging your growth and persistent efforts

Self-love is indeed a crucial foundation for personal well-being and healthy relationships with others. Let's break down some of the key aspects you mentioned:

Self-Criticism: When we lack self-love, we are more likely to engage in self-criticism and negative self-talk. This constant self-judgment can erode our self-esteem and confidence.

People-Pleasing: Without self-love, we might seek external validation and approval to compensate for the lack of self-worth. This can lead to people-pleasing behavior, where we prioritize others' needs and opinions over our own.

Perfectionism: The absence of self-love can drive perfectionism, as individuals strive to prove their worth through flawless performance. This can be exhausting and unsustainable.

Tolerating Mistreatment: People who don't value themselves may tolerate abusive or unhealthy relationships because they don't believe they deserve better.

Neglecting Needs: Self-love is about recognizing and honoring our own needs and feelings. Without it, we may neglect self-care, ignore our desires, and suppress our emotions.

Self-Sabotage: A lack of self-love can lead to self-sabotaging behaviors or decisions, as individuals may not believe they are worthy of success or happiness.

On the other hand, when we cultivate self-love:

Assertiveness: We are better able to assert ourselves and communicate our needs and boundaries effectively.

Healthy Relationships: We can establish and maintain healthy relationships built on mutual respect and understanding.

Self-Care: Self-love encourages self-care practices, which are essential for physical and mental well-being.

Pursuit of Goals: It empowers us to pursue our interests and goals with confidence and resilience.

Self-Acceptance: We can embrace our flaws and imperfections, leading to a more positive self-image.

In summary, self-love plays a pivotal role in our overall happiness and fulfillment. It enables us to navigate life's challenges with resilience, build strong connections with others, and lead a more authentic and fulfilling life. Cultivating self-love is an ongoing journey, and it often involves self-reflection, self-compassion, and the willingness to prioritize our own well-being.

In cultivating self-love, you embark on a transformative journey of self-discovery, resilience, and profound inner peace.

5. Universal Love

Beyond individual relationships, there is a concept of universal love—a love that extends to all of humanity and the world at large. This form of love involves compassion, empathy, and a desire for the well-being of all living beings. We'll explore how universal love can inspire acts of kindness, altruism, and a sense of interconnectedness with the world.

Universal love explores the idea of love as a universal, unselfish, and all-embracing force that connects all beings and transcends all barriers. Universal love can be understood and expressed in different ways, depending on one's perspective, culture, religion, or philosophy.

Universal Love: The Boundless Connection

Universal love delves into the concept of affection as an all-encompassing, selfless force that binds every living being and transcends every conceivable barrier. It is a notion that finds varied interpretations, molded by individual perspectives, cultural nuances, religious beliefs, and philosophical doctrines.

At its core, universal love represents a profound recognition of our interconnectedness with all existence. It is a force that bridges gaps, fosters empathy, and dissolves the boundaries that often divide us. This love extends beyond the confines of personal gain or desire, embracing the collective welfare of humanity and the world.

Universal love manifests in diverse ways, reflecting the richness of human thought and experience. It is a shared aspiration, regardless of cultural or spiritual backgrounds, to cultivate compassion, promote unity, and nurture the common good. It resonates in acts of kindness, altruism, and a genuine concern for the well-being of others.

Embracing universal love invites us to envision a world where divisions dissipate, prejudices crumble, and empathy thrives. It is a testament to the profound capacity of the human heart to embrace not only those closest to us but all beings, transcending barriers and fostering a global sense of interconnectedness.

Challenges and Growth in Different Forms of Love

Throughout this chapter, we'll also address the challenges and growth opportunities that each form of love presents. Whether it's navigating the complexities of romantic relationships, maintaining familial bonds in the face of adversity, nurturing deep and lasting friendships, or learning to prioritize self-care, each form of love comes with its unique set of lessons and rewards.

Love is a universal emotion that can take many forms and expressions. Different forms of love can have different challenges and opportunities for growth, depending on the nature and quality of the relationship. Some of the common forms of love are:

Platonic love: This is a type of friendship that involves a close, intimate bond without sex or romance. Platonic love can be challenging when there is a mismatch of expectations, feelings, or boundaries between the friends. Platonic love can also be affected by external factors, such as distance, time, or other relationships. Platonic love can foster growth by teaching us how to communicate, compromise, and support each other.

Romantic love: This is a type of love that involves both passion and intimacy. Passion is the intense attraction and desire that you feel for another person, while intimacy is the closeness and connection that you share with them. Romantic love can also involve commitment, which is the decision to stay with your partner and support them in the long term. Romantic love can be challenging when there is a lack of trust, respect, or compatibility between the partners. Romantic love can also change over time, depending on the circumstances and the people involved. Romantic love can foster growth by inspiring us to grow as individuals and as a couple.

Familial love: This is a type of love that is often directed at family members, whether biological, adoptive, external, or chosen. Familial love is often unconditional, meaning that you love your family members regardless of their flaws or faults. Familial love can be challenging when there is estrangement, abuse, neglect, or betrayal by family members. Familial love can also create unrealistic expectations or pressure to conform to family norms or values. Familial love can foster growth by providing us with a sense of belonging and acceptance3.

Universal love: This is a type of love that transcends all barriers and connects all beings. Universal love is unselfish and all-embracing, meaning that you love others without expecting anything in return. Universal love can be challenging when there is hatred, violence, or injustice in the world. Universal love can also be difficult to practice consistently and authentically. Universal love can foster growth by connecting us to the divine and our true nature.

These are some of the common forms of love that people experience in their lives. Each form of love has its own challenges and opportunities for growth, and each form of love can enrich our lives in different ways.

Conclusion

Love, in all its forms, enriches our lives and provides us with a profound sense of connection and purpose. As we explore the diverse manifestations of love, we gain a deeper appreciation for the tapestry of affection that weaves through our existence. Love, in its many forms, is a powerful and transformative force that continues to shape our individual journeys and collective humanity.

Chapter 6

The Alchemy of Everyday Love

Love is not solely reserved for grand gestures or momentous occasions. It resides in the everyday moments of our lives, waiting to be discovered and appreciated. In this chapter, we will explore the profound beauty of everyday love and how it can infuse our lives with meaning, joy, and a sense of connection.

1. Love in the Ordinary Moments

Everyday love is found in the seemingly mundane moments that make up our daily routines. It's the comforting touch of a loved one's hand, the shared laughter with friends, or the simple act of preparing a meal together. These ordinary moments are infused with love's magic, and when we learn to recognize and cherish them, our lives become richer.

2. The Power of Presence

One of the most potent ways to experience everyday love is through presence. Being fully present in the moment allows us to connect deeply with ourselves and others. Whether it's a heartfelt conversation with a friend or the joy of watching a sunset, being present amplifies the love and beauty in these moments.

3. Mindfulness and Gratitude

Practicing mindfulness and gratitude can help us uncover the extraordinary in the ordinary. When we cultivate awareness of our surroundings and the people in our lives, we begin to notice the love that surrounds us. By expressing gratitude for these moments, we deepen our appreciation for the love we receive and give.

4. Small Acts of Kindness

Everyday love often takes the form of small acts of kindness. It's the cup of tea your partner makes for you when you're feeling under the weather, the note of encouragement from a colleague, or the friendly gesture of a stranger. These acts may seem insignificant, but they have the power to brighten our days and strengthen our connections.

5. Love in Nature

Nature provides a magnificent canvas for experiencing everyday love. Whether it's the sight of blooming flowers, the sound of birdsong, or the feeling of a gentle breeze, the natural world offers countless opportunities to connect with love's beauty and wonder.

6. The Ripple Effect of Everyday Love

Everyday love has a ripple effect, spreading positivity and warmth not only to those directly involved but also to those who witness it. When we choose to express love in our daily lives, we inspire others to do the same. This ripple effect can contribute to creating a more compassionate and loving world.

Conclusion

The alchemy of everyday love lies in our ability to find beauty, meaning, and connection in the ordinary. By being present, cultivating mindfulness and gratitude, and embracing small acts of kindness, we can unlock the extraordinary potential of everyday love. As we continue our journey into the world of love, remember that love is not confined to grand gestures; it is woven into the very fabric of our daily existence, waiting to be discovered and celebrated.

Chapter 7

Love's Challenges and Triumphs

Love is a journey filled with both challenges and triumphs. In this chapter, we will explore the obstacles that love can encounter and the ways in which it can endure, thrive, and ultimately triumph over adversity. Understanding and navigating these challenges is essential for fostering healthy, lasting relationships and experiencing the extraordinary resilience of love.

1. The Nature of Challenges in Love

Love, while beautiful and transformative, is not without its difficulties. It often involves navigating complex emotions, communication breakdowns, and external pressures. Recognizing the inevitability of challenges in love is the first step in addressing and overcoming them.

2. Communication and Understanding

Effective communication is the cornerstone of any successful relationship. Misunderstandings, conflicts, and unspoken expectations can strain even the most profound love connections. We will explore strategies for improving communication and deepening mutual understanding.

3. Trust and Vulnerability

Trust is the bedrock of love, and vulnerability is its companion. Opening up to another person and exposing our true selves can be both beautiful and terrifying. We will delve into the importance of trust and the power of vulnerability in building and maintaining strong relationships.

4. External Pressures

Love often faces external pressures, whether from societal expectations, cultural differences, or life's challenges. These pressures can test the strength of a relationship and require couples to adapt and grow together. We will explore how love can triumph over these external obstacles.

5. Forgiveness and Healing

Love is not immune to mistakes, hurt, or betrayal. Forgiveness and the process of healing are vital for repairing relationships after they've faced hardship. We will discuss the power of forgiveness and the journey toward healing in the context of love.

6. Love's Resilience

Despite the challenges it encounters, love has an extraordinary resilience. It has the power to overcome adversity, rebuild trust, and emerge stronger than before. We will examine stories of love that have endured through thick and thin, showcasing love's remarkable ability to triumph over obstacles.

7. Lessons from Love's Challenges

The challenges we face in love often hold valuable lessons. They can teach us about ourselves, our partners, and the nature of love itself. By embracing these challenges as opportunities for growth, we can navigate the complexities of love with greater wisdom and compassion.

Conclusion

Love's journey is not a straight path; it is marked by twists, turns, and occasional hurdles. However, it is precisely through facing and overcoming these challenges that love grows deeper and more profound. As we continue to explore the extraordinary nature of love, remember that love's triumphs often shine brightest in the face of adversity.

Chapter 8

The Alchemy of Long-lasting Love

Long-lasting love is a testament to the enduring power of this extraordinary force. In this chapter, we will delve into the secrets and qualities that underpin love that stands the test of time. From the initial spark to the decades of commitment, long-lasting love is a remarkable journey filled with wisdom and enduring connection.

1. The Foundation of Long-lasting Love

Long-lasting love is built on a solid foundation of trust, communication, and shared values. It begins with a spark of attraction but evolves into something deeper and more profound. We will explore the qualities that contribute to the lasting nature of love.

2. Navigating Life's Seasons Together

A significant aspect of long-lasting love is the ability to navigate life's seasons together. Couples must adapt and grow as individuals and as partners. We will discuss how couples evolve and support each other through life's challenges and milestones.

3. The Art of Compromise

Successful long-term relationships often involve compromise. Balancing individual needs and desires with those of a partner is a delicate art. We will explore the importance of compromise in maintaining harmony and satisfaction in relationships.

4. Maintaining Passion and Intimacy

As time passes, maintaining passion and intimacy can become a challenge. We will discuss strategies for keeping the spark alive and nurturing physical and emotional closeness in long-lasting relationships.

5. Weathering Storms Together

Long-lasting love is not immune to difficulties. Couples may face financial struggles, health crises, or the loss of loved ones. We will examine how enduring love provides the strength and resilience to weather life's storms together.

6. Celebrating Milestones and Traditions

Creating and celebrating milestones and traditions can strengthen the bond in long-lasting love. These rituals offer opportunities for connection and reflection on the journey as a couple. We will explore the significance of such shared experiences.

7. Wisdom from Couples

Throughout this chapter, we will hear from couples who have sustained their love over the years. Their stories and insights will shed light on the joys and challenges of long-lasting love, offering inspiration and guidance.

8. The Legacy of Long-lasting Love

Long-lasting love leaves a lasting legacy. It impacts not only the individuals involved but also future generations. We will reflect on how enduring love shapes families, communities, and society as a whole.

Conclusion

Long-lasting love is a profound and beautiful journey that requires commitment, adaptability, and a deep understanding of each other. As we conclude this exploration of love's extraordinary nature, remember that love's enduring quality is a testament to its transformative power and its ability to enrich our lives in ways that are truly extraordinary.

Chapter 9

Love's Legacy

Love leaves an indelible mark on our lives and the world around us. In this chapter of our journey into the extraordinary nature of love, we will reflect on the lasting impact of love and how it creates a legacy of kindness, compassion, and positive change.

1. The Ripple Effect of Love

Love has a ripple effect that extends far beyond the individuals directly involved. Acts of love and kindness have the power to inspire others, creating a chain reaction of goodwill. We will explore how love's ripple effect spreads positivity and enriches the lives of countless others.

2. Love's Influence on Relationships

The love we experience in our relationships often shapes our attitudes and behaviors in all areas of life. We will examine how healthy love relationships serve as models for empathy, communication, and respect, impacting not only partners but also children, friends, and colleagues.

3. Love in the Community

Love is not confined to personal relationships; it also plays a vital role in building strong, caring communities. We will discuss how love fosters a sense of belonging, social cohesion, and collective well-being within communities.

4. Love's Impact on Society

On a broader scale, love has the potential to transform societies. Acts of love and altruism can drive positive social change, inspire movements, and address societal issues. We will explore how love has been a driving force in history and continues to shape the world today.

5. Love as a Source of Inspiration

Love inspires artists, writers, musicians, and creators of all kinds. We will delve into how love's beauty and complexity have been a wellspring of inspiration throughout human history, resulting in timeless works of art, literature, and music.

6. Love's Role in Nurturing Future Generations

As parents and caregivers, our capacity to love and nurture has a profound impact on the upbringing and well-being of future generations. We will discuss the importance of passing on values of love, empathy, and compassion to children, shaping a brighter future.

7. The Enduring Legacy of Love

Throughout this chapter, we will explore stories of individuals whose love has left a lasting legacy. These stories serve as reminders of the profound and far-reaching impact of love on our world.

Conclusion

Love's legacy is not measured in material wealth or worldly success but in the lives touched, the hearts warmed, and the positive change it brings to individuals, communities, and society as a whole. As we conclude our exploration of love, may we carry forward the understanding that love's legacy endures, and each act of love contributes to a more compassionate and interconnected world.

About the Author

Ujunwa Miriam Ekeh is a dynamic individual whose journey through life has been marked by a unique blend of academic achievement, creative passion, and civic engagement. With a Higher National Diploma(HND) in Public Administration from Abia State Polytechnic, Aba, she has honed her knowledge and skills in the realm of public governance.

However, Ujunwa's story transcends the confines of her academic pursuits. She possesses a boundless passion for the world of fashion design, a passion that has ignited her creative spirit and allowed her to explore the depths of self-expression through clothing and style.

Beyond her love for fashion, Ujunwa Miriam Ekeh serves as an ad-hoc staff member of the Independent National Electoral Commission (INEC). Her involvement in this critical civic duty reflects her commitment to ensuring the integrity of democratic processes in her community.

Ujunwa is not only defined by her educational and professional achievements but also by her unyielding dedication to personal growth, community service, and artistic expression. She embodies the spirit of a multi-talented and compassionate individual who is constantly evolving and seeking new ways to contribute to the world around her.

Her unique blend of academic rigor, artistic flair, and civic responsibility is a testament to her well-rounded character and the boundless potential that she brings to every aspect of her life. As she embarks on this literary journey into the exploration of love, Ujunwa Miriam Ekeh's rich and diverse experiences promise to bring a unique perspective and depth to her writing, offering readers a chance to connect with her passion, insight, and dedication to the subject matter.

Self-love is not always easy to practice, especially when we face difficulties or criticism from others or ourselves. Sometimes we may need some guidance or inspiration to cultivate self-love in our lives.

References

Arendt, Hannah (1996). Love and St. Augustine.
Chicago, IL: The University of Chicago Press.
Augustine (1955). Treatises on marriage and other
subjects. Roy J. Deferrari (Ed.). Washington, DC:
Catholic University of America Press.
Augustine (1960). The confessions of Saint Augustine
(John K. Ryan, Trans.). New York, NY: Image Books.
Augustine (1994a). The city of God (Marcus Dods,
trans.). Peabody, MA: Hendrickson Publishers.

Augustine (1994b). On Christian doctrine. In Philip Schaff (Ed.), A select library of the Nicene and post-Nicene fathers. Peabody, MA: Hendrickson Publishers.

Boylan, Michael (2011). Duties to children. In Michael Boylan (Ed.), The morality and global justice reader (385–405). Boulder, CO: Westview.

Cranston, Maurice (1991). Jean-Jacques: The early life and work of Jean-Jacques Rousseau, 1712–1754. Chicago, IL: The University of Chicago Press.

Feinberg, M (1980). The child's right to an open future. In W. Aiken & H. LaFollette (Eds.), Whose child? Children's rights, parental authority, and state power (124–153). New Jersey, NJ: Littlefield, Adams, & Co.

Freud, Sigmund (1913). Totem und tabu: Einige übereinstimmungen im seelenleben der wilden und der neurotiker [Totem and Taboo: Resemblances between the Psychic Lives of Savages and Neurotics]. Leipzig, Germany: Hugo Heller.

Freud, Sigmund (2000). Three essays on the theory of sexuality (James Strachey, trans.). New York, NY: Basic Books.

Grimsley, Ronald (1973). The philosophy of Rousseau. Oxford, United Kingdom: Oxford University Press.

Guthrie, W. K. C. (1956). Plato: Protagoras and Meno. London, United Kingdom: Sage.

Kirk, Geoffrey S., & Raven, John E. (1984). The presocratic philosophers. Cambridge, United Kingdom: Cambridge University Press.

Kingsley, Peter (1995). Ancient philosophy, mystery, and magic: Empedocles and Pythagorean tradition. Oxford, United Kingdom: Oxford University Press.

Kant, Immanuel (2003). Utemeljitev metafizike nravnosti [The metaphysics of morals]. Ljubljana, Slovenia: Založba ZRC.

Lacan, Jacques (1994). Sections from his work on transference. Filozofija skozi psihoanalizo [Philosophy through psychoanalysis]. Ljubljana, Slovenia: Analecta.

Liao, S. Matthew (2006a). The idea of a duty to love. Journal of Value Inquiry 40(1): 1–22.

Liao, S. Matthew (2006b). The right of children to be loved. Journal of Political Philosophy 14(4), 420–440.

Liao, S. Matthew (2012). Why children need to be loved. Critical Review of International Social and Political Philosophy 15(3), 347–358.

Martin, Alain, & Primavesi, Oliver (1998). L'Empédocle de Strasbourg (P. Strasb. gr. Inv. 1665–1666). Berlin, Germany: Walter de Gruyter.

Nussbaum, Martha (1986). The fragility of goodness: Luck and ethics in Greek tragedy and philosophy. Cambridge, United Kingdom: Cambridge University Press.

Nussbaum, Martha (2001). Upheavals of Thought: The intelligence of emotions. New York, NY: Cambridge University Press. Nygren, Anders (1953). Agape and Eros. London, United Kingdom: S.P.C.K.

Plato (1960). Symposium (S. Groden, trans.). Amherst, MA: University of Massachusetts Press.

Plato (1963). Eutyphro and Phaedrus. In Edith Hamilton & Huntington Cairns (Eds.), The collected dialogues. Princeton, NJ: Princeton University Press.

Rousseau, Jean Jacques (1979). Emile: Or on education (Allan Bloom, trans.). London, United Kingdom: Basic Books.

Rousseau, Jean Jacques (1997). Julie, or the new Heloise: Letters of two lovers who live in a small town at the foot of the Alps (Philip Stewart, trans.). Lebanon, NH: University Press of New England.
Spinoza, Baruch (1992). The Ethics (Seymour Feldman, trans.). Indianapolis, IN: Hackett.
Starobinski, Jean (1988). Jean-Jacques Rousseau: Transparency and obstruction. Chicago, IL: University of Chicago Press.
Tobler, Waldo (1970). A computer movie simulating urban growth in the Detroit region. Economic Geography, 46(2), 234–240.
Verhaeghe, Paul (1999). Love in a time of loneliness. London, United Kingdom: Rebus.

(1) Sternberg's Triangular Theory of Love - Verywell Mind. https://www.verywellmind.com/types-of-love-we-experience-2303200.
(2) Learn the Different Types of Love (and Better Understand ... - Lifehack. https://www.lifehack.org/816195/types-of-love.
(3) 8 Kinds of Love and Our 5 Love Languages – Cleveland Clinic. https://health.clevelandclinic.org/understanding-love-stages-and-languages/.
(4) Sufjan Stevens – Mystery of Love Lyrics | Genius Lyrics. https://genius.com/Sufjan-stevens-mystery-of-love-lyrics.
(5) "Mystery of Love" by Sufjan Stevens from the Call Me By Your Name .... https://www.youtube.com/watch?v=KQT32vW61eI.
(6) Mystery of Love - Wikipedia. https://en.wikipedia.org/wiki/Mystery_of_Love.

(7) Mystery of Love Sufjan Stevens.
https://tv.sohu.com/v/dXMvMzM4NDUwMjIzLzI4
MTc2MTQ5NC5zaHRtbA==.html.
(8) mystery of love.
https://www.bilibili.com/video/BV1m84y1774Z/?uid
=4256316D3834793137345A.

(9) 【Vox Akuma】 Blessed be the mystery of love.
https://www.bilibili.com/video/BV14M4y1Q73C/?uid
=425631344D347931513733343.
(10) undefined.
https://www.facebook.com/CallMeByYour.
(10) What Is Romantic Love? - Verywell Mind.
https://www.verywellmind.com/what-is-romantic-
love-2303236.
(11) Romantic Love: Meaning, Signs, Types, Drawbacks
and   More   -   MantraCare.
https://mantracare.org/therapy/what-is/romantic-
love/.
(12)   Romance   (love)   -   Wikipedia.
https://en.wikipedia.org/wiki/Romance_%28love%29.
(`13)   Healing   -   Wikipedia.
https://en.wikipedia.org/wiki/Healing.
(14) Physical Healing: Laying of Hands and the Power
of   Faith   -   Egely   Wheel.
https://egelywheel.net/physical-healing/.

9 798862 576030